If you were a

TRIANGLE

by Marcie Aboff
illustrated by Sarah Dillard

Picture Window Books
Minneapolis, Minnesota

Editor: Jill Kalz
Designer: Lori Bye
Page Production: Melissa Kes
Art Director: Nathan Gassman
Editorial Director: Nick Healy
Creative Director: Joe Ewest
The illustrations in this book were created with watercolor and gouache.

Picture Window Books
151 Good Counsel Drive
P.O. Box 669
Mankato, MN 56002-0669
877-845-8392
www.picturewindowbooks.com

Printed in the United States of America.

 All books published by Picture Window Books
are manufactured with paper containing
at least 10 percent post-consumer waste.

Library of Congress Cataloging-in-Publication Data
Aboff, Marcie.
If you were a triangle / by Marcie Aboff ; illustrated by
Sarah Dillard.
p. cm. — (Math fun)
Includes index.
ISBN 978-1-4048-5513-7 (library binding)
ISBN 978-1-4048-5688-2 (paperback)
1. Triangle—Juvenile literature. 2. Shapes—Juvenile
literature. I. Dillard, Sarah, 1961- ill. II. Title.
QA482.A26 2010
516'.154—dc22
                                        2009006891

Special thanks to our adviser for his expertise:

Stuart Farm, M.Ed., Mathematics Lecturer
University of North Dakota

triangle—a flat, closed figure with three straight sides

If you were a triangle ...

... you could be seen on the street,

YIELD

4

in a band,

or at the kitchen table.

5

If you were a triangle, you would always have three sides.
Your sides would be straight.

The monkeys swing from the triangles.

6

The camels play hide-and-seek around the pyramids. Each slanted face of a pyramid looks like a triangle.

If you were a triangle, you would be a three-sided polygon. A polygon is a flat, closed figure with three or more straight sides.

NON-POLYGON PATTERNS

Lulu shops for new wallpaper. She likes the polygon patterns.

She picks the one with blue and purple triangles.

If you were a triangle, you would have three corners.

Hannah enters the Triangle Bike Race.
Her friends gather at each corner to cheer her on.

If you were a triangle, you would have three angles.
An angle is the measurement between two sides at a corner.

Six cattle graze in a triangle-shaped yard.

Two spotted cows graze in one angle.

Two brown cows graze in another angle.

And two tan cows graze in another angle.

If you were a triangle, you could be a right triangle.
Two of your sides would be perpendicular to one another.
One side would stand straight up from the other side lying flat.
Those two sides would form a right angle.

Oh, no! It's nine o'clock.
Hunter is late for school again!

If you were a triangle, you could be an isosceles triangle. Two of your sides would be the same length. Your third side would be a different length.

Dipsy and Dot can't wait to eat their ice cream.

But Dipsy trips and drops her cone.
Dot's cone drips all over her dress.

If you were a triangle, you could be an equilateral triangle. Your three sides would be the same length.

Bo plays the triangle, Ben plays the drums, and Bea plays the keyboard.

Their music shakes the roof!

If you were a triangle, you could put two of you together to form another shape.

Grace puts together two right triangles of the same size and makes a rectangle.

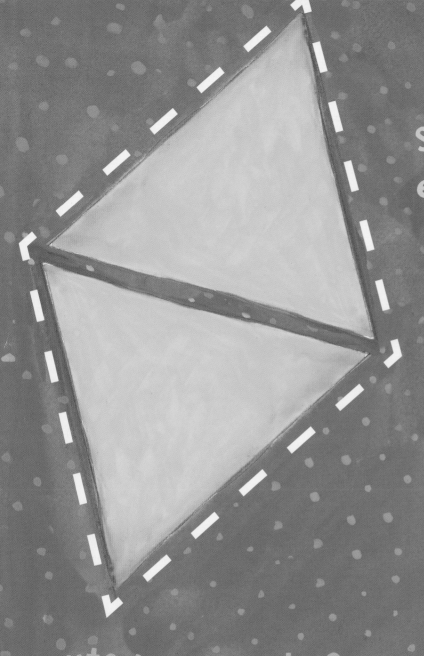

She puts together two equilateral triangles of the same size and makes a diamond.

She puts together two isosceles right triangles of the same size and makes a square.

21

You could be breakfast, lunch, and dinner ...

... if you were a triangle.

WHAT KIND OF TRIANGLE AM I?

Now that you know three different kinds of triangles, look at the triangles below. Which ones are right triangles? Which ones are isosceles triangles? Which ones are equilateral triangles? Check your answers below.

1.
2.
3.
4.
5.
6.

Answers: 4, 6 right; 3, 4, 5 isosceles; 2 equilateral; note that triangle 4 is both an isosceles and a right (called an isosceles right triangle), and triangle 1 is none of the a

23

Glossary

angle—the measurement between two sides at a corner

diamond—a flat, closed figure with four sides of equal length and
opposite angles of equal measure

equilateral triangle—a triangle with three sides of equal length

isosceles triangle—a triangle with two sides of equal length

perpendicular—one side standing straight up from another side
lying flat, forming a right angle

polygon—a flat, closed figure with three or more straight sides

rectangle—a flat, closed figure with four sides and four right angles

right angle—an angle formed by two perpendicular sides

right triangle—a triangle with two perpendicular sides

square—a flat, closed figure with four sides of equal length and
four right angles

triangle—a flat, closed figure with three straight sides

To Learn More

More Books to Read

Burns, Marilyn. *The Greedy Triangle.* New York: Scholastic, 2008.

Lorbiecki, Marybeth. *Triangles.* Edina, Minn.: Magic Wagon, 2008.

Internet Sites

FactHound offers a safe, fun way to find Internet sites
related to this book. All of the sites on FactHound have
been researched by our staff.

Here's all you do:
Visit *www.facthound.com*
FactHound will fetch the best sites for you!

Index

Look for all of the books in the Math Fun series:

If You Were a Circle

If You Were a Divided-by Sign

If You Were a Fraction

If You Were a Minus Sign

If You Were a Minute

If You Were a Plus Sign

If You Were a Polygon

If You Were a Pound or a Kilogram

If You Were a Quadrilateral

If You Were a Quart or a Liter

If You Were a Set

If You Were a Times Sign

If You Were a Triangle

If You Were an Even Number

If You Were an Inch or a Centimeter

If You Were an Odd Number